Designs and Patterns
for Embroiderers and Craftsmen

Designs and Patterns
for Embroiderers and Craftsmen

512 Motifs from the Wm. Briggs and Company Ltd.
"Album of Transfer Patterns"

Edited by
Marion Nichols

DOVER PUBLICATIONS, INC.

NEW YORK

Published in Canada by General Publishing Company, Ltd., 30 Lesmill Road, Don Mills, Toronto, Ontario.
Published in the United Kingdom by Constable and Company, Ltd., 10 Orange Street, London WC 2.

This Dover edition, first published in 1974, is a selection from the Wm. Briggs and Company Ltd. *Album of Transfer Patterns* [n.d., circa 1900?]. This Dover edition contains an introduction with instructions for transferring designs and a description of embroidery stitches by Marion Nichols.

International Standard Book Number: 0-486-23030-9
Library of Congress Catalog Card Number: 73-93081

Manufactured in the United States of America
Dover Publications, Inc.
180 Varick Street
New York, N.Y. 10014

INTRODUCTION

This collection of the fine turn-of-the-century embroidery designs has been edited and published especially for the needleworker who is looking for something more artistically valid than what is customarily available. Originally intended to be used on table mats, dresser scarfs and "D'Oylies," these designs are eminently suitable as decorations on pillows, eyeglass cases, handbags, blue jeans and dozens of other objects in constant use today. However, many of the designs are so attractive and carefully worked out that they are very successful simply as pictures to be framed and hung.

As rich and varied as this archive is, happily you are not limited simply to choosing and executing a single design. In fact, one of the best features of the collection is that the designs complement each other beautifully, and thereby invite you to invent your own composition by combining elements from different plates. What a boon for you needleworkers who have always wanted to try your hand at an original design but have not quite been able to pull it off successfully! Try again, using a floral motif from here, leaves or stem from there, a butterfly or a bird from still another plate, and soon your own needle-painting will begin to form. Add your personal color scheme and appropriate stitches from your repertory, and you will have the satisfaction of creating a truly original design. After you have created several compositions from this material, you may find yourself in the enviable position of being able to design completely on your own, even though you may never have dreamed this possible!

The Table of Contents of this volume is organized according to motif, size and shape, and *suggested* uses. We emphasize "suggested" because we hope you will feel free to use your own imagination in order to get the designs to work for you.

This is primarily a sourcebook of designs and design ideas, and so we do not attempt to cover the fascinating intricacies of the craft itself, which are now well described in numerous publications. However, we do want to explain how to transfer designs to fabric as well as to illustrate several basic stitches and offer a few suggestions on how to make the best use of them.

After you have chosen the design and decided upon its purpose, select and prepare the background fabric. Choose a fabric that is compatible with the design and suitable for the intended use. Pictures that are to be framed and hung on a wall may never have to be washed or take hard wear, and so can be done on delicate fabrics; but drapes or pillows will get soiled and so require sturdier material. If you are not sure of the washability of a fabric, test a small piece before you spend valuable time embroidering it. Remember that a test by gentle handwashing in cold water with special soap does not necessarily mean that the finished piece can be tossed into the washer with the family wash! After determining suitability and/or washability, make sure the fabric is clean and pressed. Avoid using materials from which you are unable to remove creases; a crease which does not iron out before the embroidering will remain to infuriate you later.

Next, cut the fabric to size, being careful to allow for seams, hems or the fold-over necessary if you plan to mount the piece. Make sure the cuts are "on the straight" of the fabric by pulling out a guide thread in each direction and then cutting along these lines; do not depend upon a ruler line since the fabric may have been pulled out of shape. If a piece is still out of square after cutting, take the time to dampen and press it over again. You'll be glad you did! If the fabric ravels badly, it is wise to whip the edges by hand with an overcast stitch or run a large zigzag machine stitch along the edges.

Once you have chosen a design and fabric for a project, follow these simple steps to bring your work to a successful conclusion:

Step 1. Gather the materials needed for transferring and embroidering.
 You will need:

 Tracing paper
 Large piece of cardboard (oak tag or tablet back)
 Straight pins
 Tracing wheel, dull pencil or other stylus
 Ruler
 Dressmaker's carbon paper (in a color that contrasts with the color of the fabric)
 Flat smooth surface (such as a table)
 Background fabric
 Threads (yarns) for embroidery
 Embroidery tools (frame, needles, thimble, scissors, etc.)

BASIC EMBROIDERY STITCHES ARRANGED BY USES

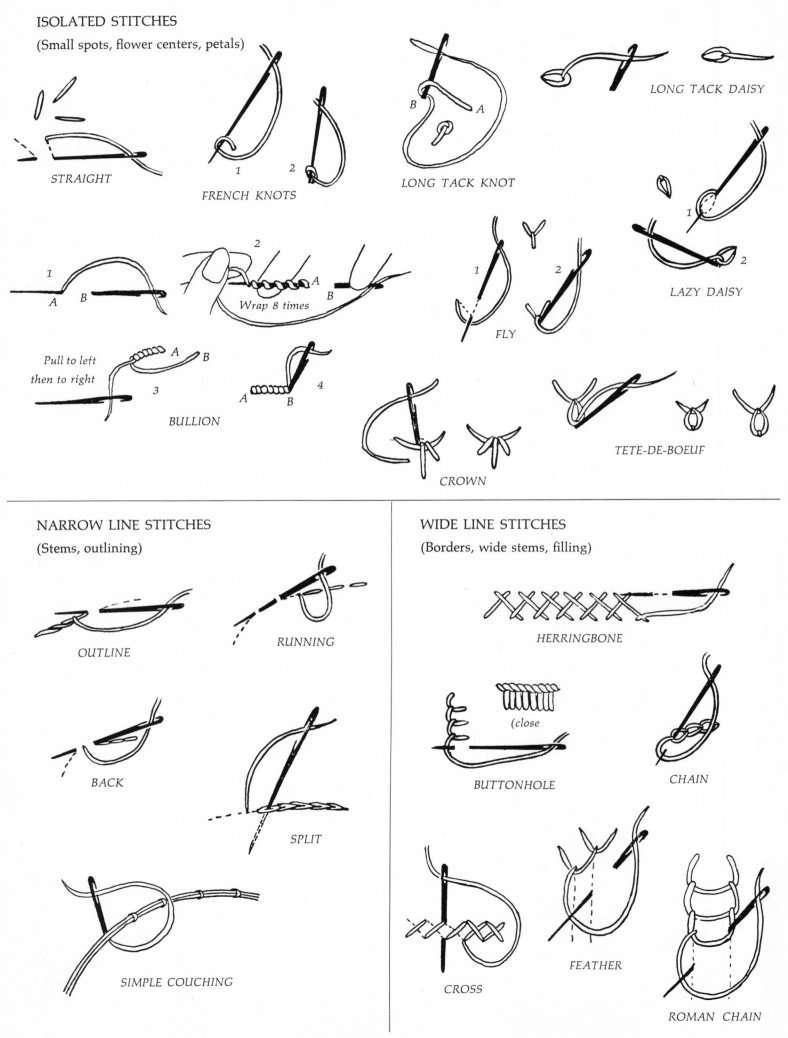

ISOLATED STITCHES
(Small spots, flower centers, petals)

STRAIGHT

FRENCH KNOTS
1   2

LONG TACK KNOT
B   A

LONG TACK DAISY

LAZY DAISY
1   2

FLY
1   2

1   2
A   B
Wrap 8 times   A   B

Pull to left
then to right
3   A   B

BULLION
A   B   4

CROWN

TETE-DE-BOEUF

NARROW LINE STITCHES
(Stems, outlining)

OUTLINE

RUNNING

BACK

SPLIT

SIMPLE COUCHING

WIDE LINE STITCHES
(Borders, wide stems, filling)

HERRINGBONE

BUTTONHOLE
(close

CHAIN

CROSS

FEATHER

ROMAN CHAIN

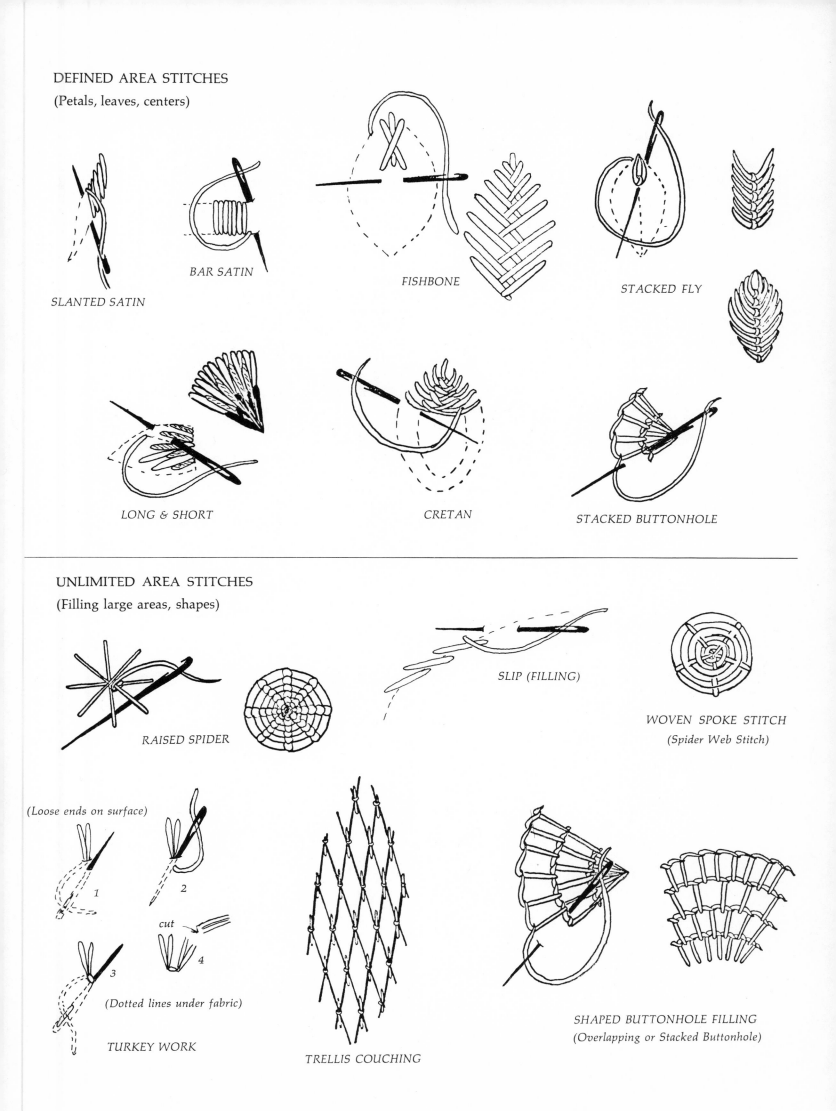

DEFINED AREA STITCHES
(Petals, leaves, centers)

SLANTED SATIN

BAR SATIN

FISHBONE

STACKED FLY

LONG & SHORT

CRETAN

STACKED BUTTONHOLE

UNLIMITED AREA STITCHES
(Filling large areas, shapes)

RAISED SPIDER

SLIP (FILLING)

WOVEN SPOKE STITCH
(Spider Web Stitch)

(Loose ends on surface)

1

2

cut

3

4

(Dotted lines under fabric)

TURKEY WORK

TRELLIS COUCHING

SHAPED BUTTONHOLE FILLING
(Overlapping or Stacked Buttonhole)

Step 2. Make a tracing by putting a sheet of tracing paper over the design and drawing over each line with a lead pencil. We do not advise tracing directly from the book onto the fabric because the page might tear and render the designs on the overleaf page unusable.

Step 3. Transfer the design. Place the cardboard on a flat surface; this not only protects the surface of the table from scarring under the pressure of the tracing wheel but also provides the firm padding under the fabric necessary to produce a smooth line. Carefully position your tracing on the fabric and pin it at the four corners. If the design is to be centered, use a ruler to determine the midpoint.

Before we proceed with the transfer process, let me say a word about carbon papers. Do *not* use typewriter carbon; it will smudge and rub off on the fabric and is almost impossible to remove. Dressmaker's carbon, available at notions, fabric and dime stores, comes in packs of assorted colors in strips about 7 x 20 inches. It has a hard waxy finish and is designed for our purpose.

Slip the carbon, color-side down, between the tracing and the fabric, temporarily removing one of the corner pins if necessary. Do not pin the carbon in place. With a hard, even pressure, trace a few lines with a tracing wheel or similar tool. Raise one corner of the tracing and the carbon to check the impression. If the results are too faint, apply more pressure; if too heavy, less pressure. Too heavy a line is difficult to hide with embroidery and too light a line is hard to see, but keep in mind that the transfer does have a tendency to fade a bit as it is handled and so should be a little on the heavy side. After adjusting the impression, trace the entire design and then remove the carbon and all but two pins. Carefully lift one side of the tracing paper and check to make sure the design is intact on the fabric *before removing the pattern.* Once removed it is almost impossible to register the pattern to the fabric again.

If later on, during the embroidery process, the line becomes too faint, touch it up with a waterproof felt-tip pen or a laundry marker. Test the pen! If it is not waterproof it will run and ruin your embroidery; just the moisture from a steam iron is enough to cause this. (A pencil can be used unless you are working with light-colored yarns which the lead could discolor.)

That's all there is to the basic method of transferring designs. You are now ready to embroider. Keep in mind that the success of your embroidery depends, like a good marriage, on the compatibility of its component parts—a happy wedding of design, fabric, thread and stitches, and most of all, your loving efforts.

CONTENTS
and Index of Uses

Designs and Patterns
for Embroiderers and Craftsmen

Hawthorn

Ivy and Forget-Me-Not

Daisy and Forget-Me-Not

Fuchsia and Heather

Wild Rose

Geranium

Wallflower

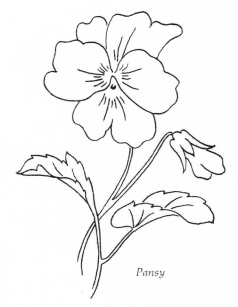

Pansy

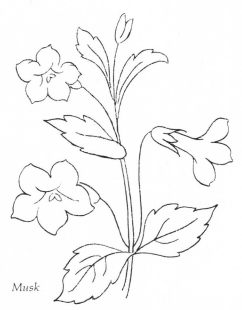

Musk

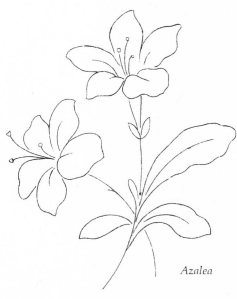

Azalea

Snowdrops

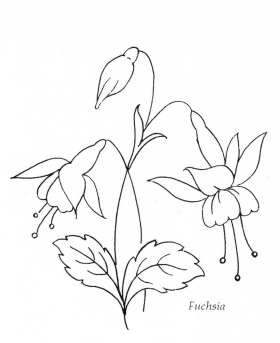

Fuchsia

Briar Rose

Apple Blossom

Lilac

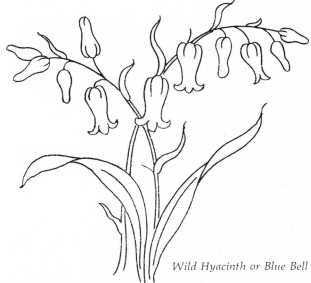

Wild Hyacinth or Blue Bell

Strawberries

Oak Leaf and Acorn

Chestnut

Rushes

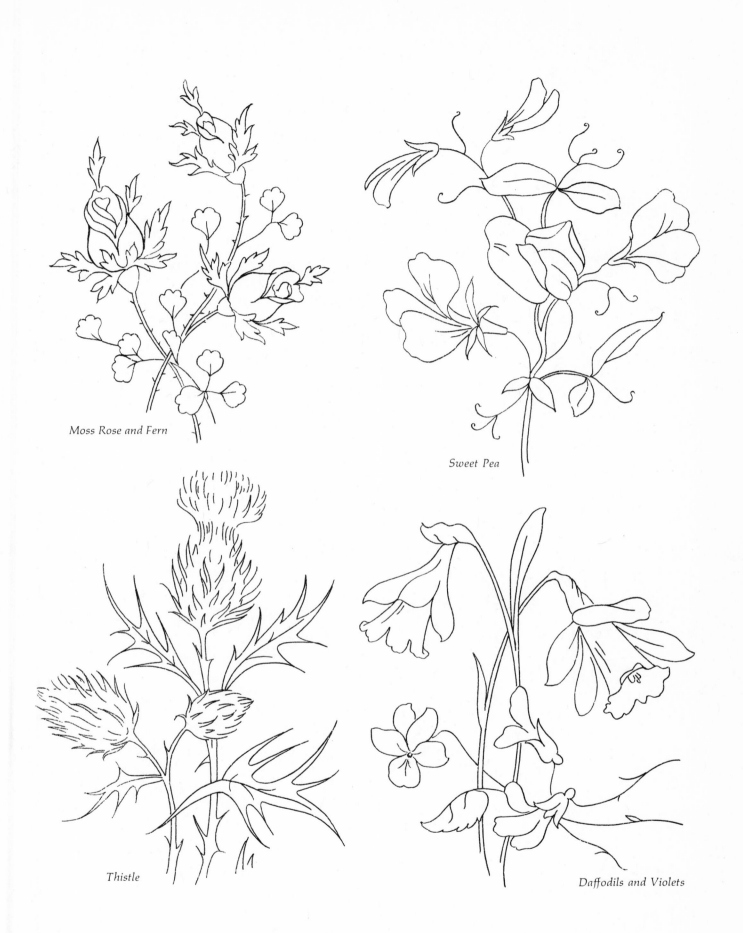

Moss Rose and Fern

Sweet Pea

Thistle

Daffodils and Violets

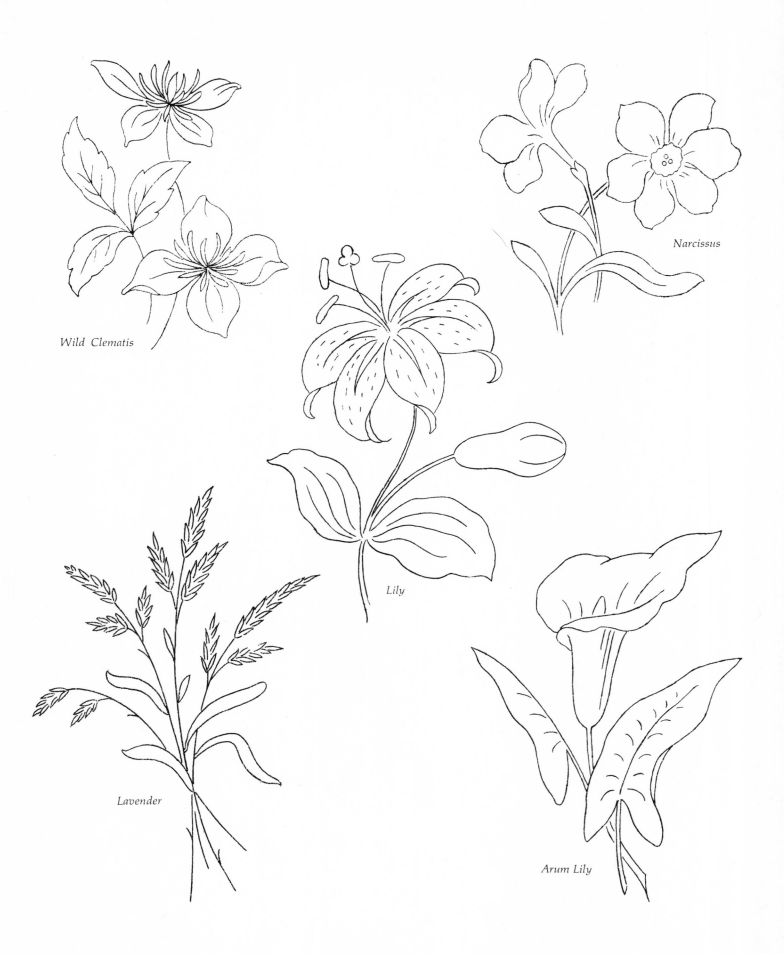

Wild Clematis

Narcissus

Lily

Lavender

Arum Lily

Rhododendron

Orchid

Vine

Convolvulus

Begonia

Chrysanthemum

Daisy

Poppy

Arum Lily

Thistle

Marigold

Chestnut

Poppy

Cornflower

Japanese Lily

Narcissus

Poppy

Tulip

Pansy

Daffodil

Daisies

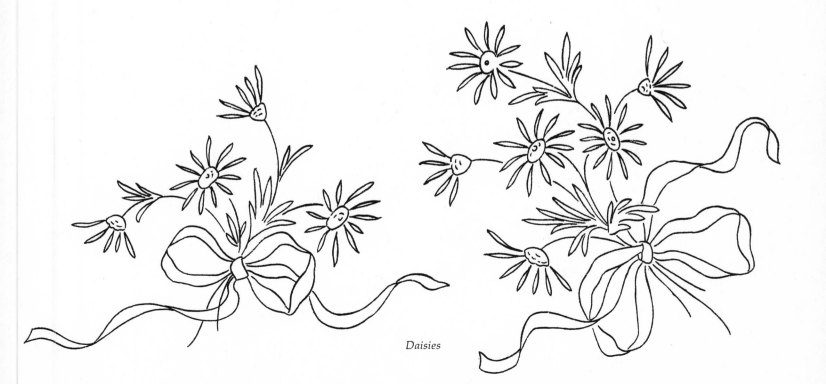

Daisies

Daffodil

Water Lily

Dwarf Sunflower

Pansy

Flowering Rush

Daffodil

Lilac

Chrysanthemum

Wild Rose and Jessamine

Tiger Lily

Virginian Creeper

Picotee and Basket

Wild Rose

Daisy

Poppy

Marguerite

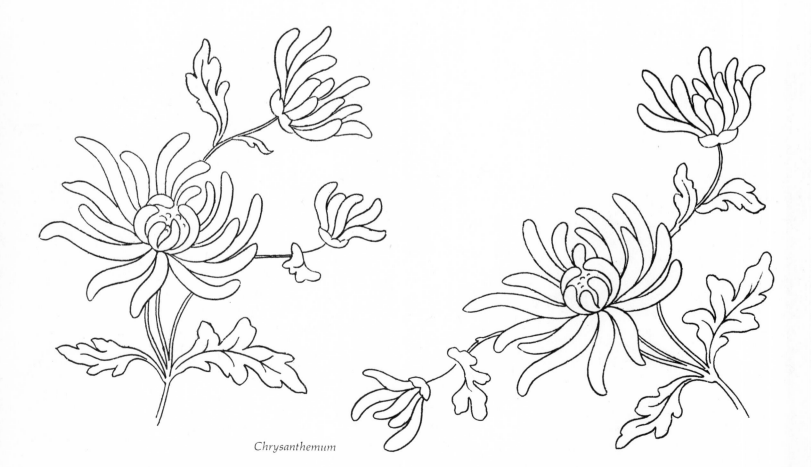

Chrysanthemum

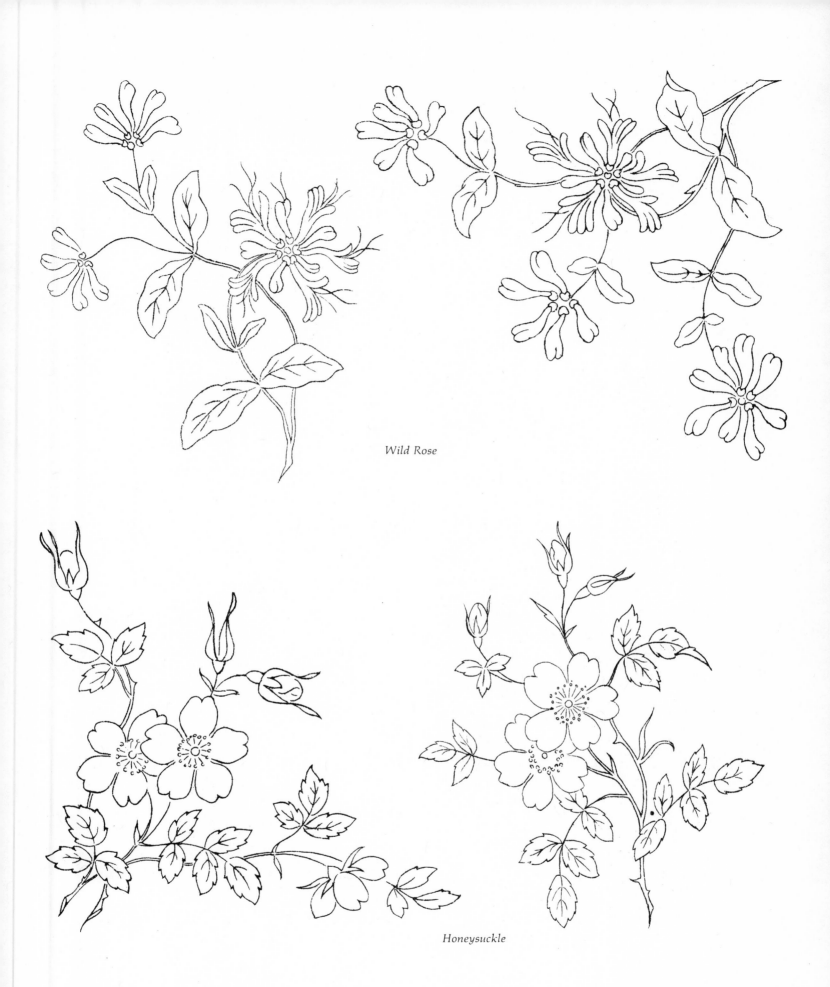

Wild Rose

Honeysuckle

Arum Lily

Wild Rose and Jessamine

Tiger Lily

Azalea and Fern

Lilac

Carnation

Daisy

Passion Flower

Cornflower and Wheat

Rosebud and Forget-Me-Not

Forget-Me-Not and Fern

Narcissus

Iris

Thistle

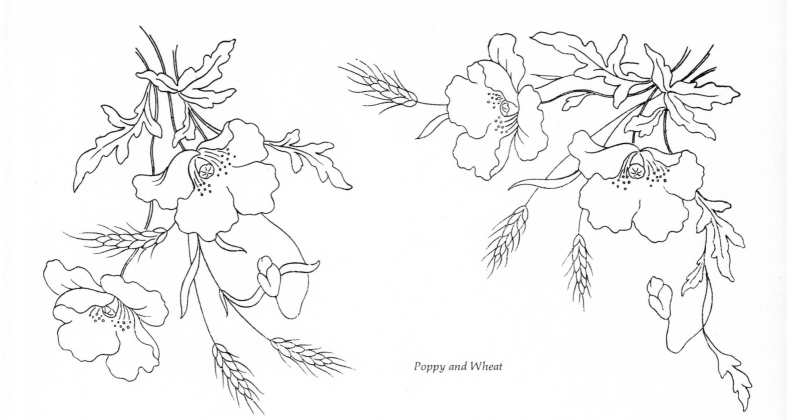

Poppy and Wheat

Garden Rose

Sunflower

Daisy

Single Dahlia

Carnation

Pansy and Fern

Chrysanthemum

Daffodil

Tulip

Tulip

Single   Peony

Single Peony

Gladiola

Gladiola

Single Dahlia

Single Dahlia

Sunflower

Sunflower

Tiger Lily

Tiger Lily

Marguerite

Marguerite

Poppy

Poppy

Poppy

Pansy

"Hungarian" Quilt Square

"Hungarian" Quilt Square

Quilt Square

Quilt Square

"Oriental" Quilt Square

"Oriental" Quilt Square

Lotus

Japanese Quince

Marguerite

Cornflower

"Hungarian" Quilt Square

"Hungarian" Quilt Square

Sunflowers

Almond Blossoms

Tulips

Carnations

Poppies

Cabbage Roses

"Oriental" Cushion Square

Yellow Asters

"Silistrian" Cushion Square

"Chinese" Cushion Square

"Thuringia" Cushion Square

"Nikita" Cushion Square

"Russian Cross Stitch" Quilt Square

"Russian Cross Stitch" Quilt Square

Pimpernel

Forget-Me-Not

Ox-Eye Daisy and Forget-Me-Not

Apple Blossom

Field Daisy and Fern

Ivy

Rosebuds and Fern

Poppy and Wheat

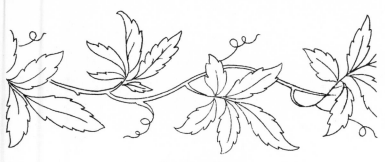

Virginian Creeper

Wild Rose

Fuchsia

Mountain Ash

Jasmine

Jasmine and Rosebud

Wild Rose and Jasmine

Virginian Creeper

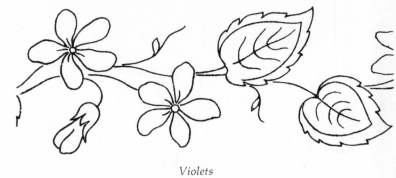

Rosebud

Violets

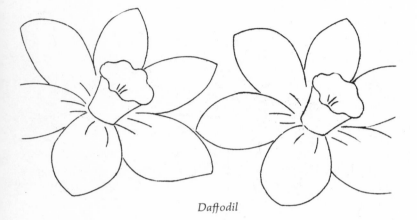

Daffodil

Narcissus

Marguerite

Maidenhair Fern

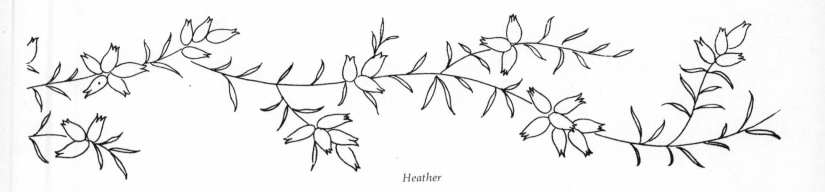

Heather

Wild Pansy

Shamrock

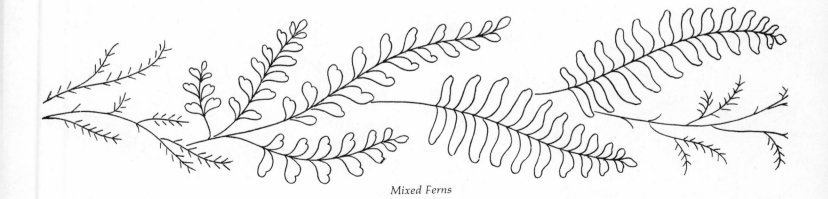

Mixed Ferns

Chrysanthemums

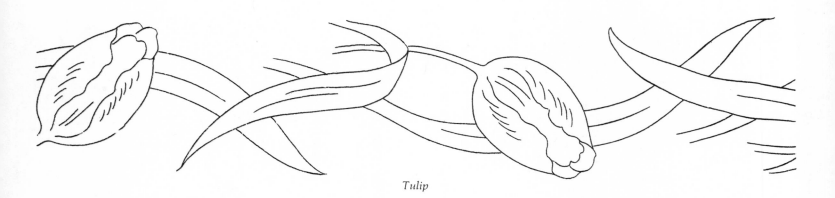

Tulip

Buttercup

Wild Rose and Forget-Me-Nots

Cornflower, Poppy Bud and Wheat

Violets

Hawthorn

Ivy and Forget-Me-Nots

Chrysanthemum

Single Dahlia

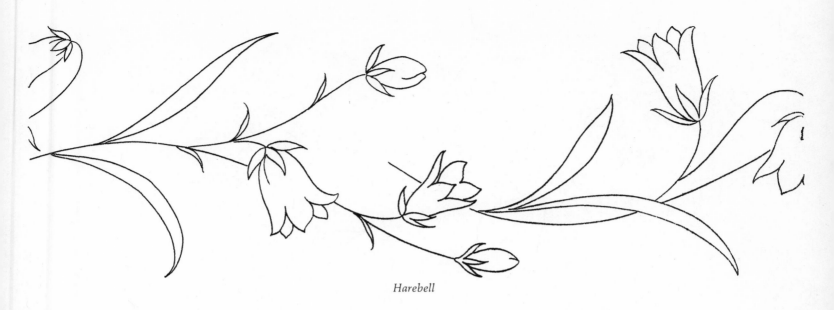

Harebell

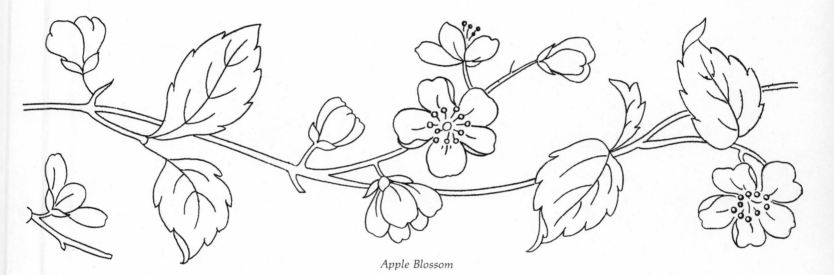

Apple Blossom

Strawberries

Chrysanthemum

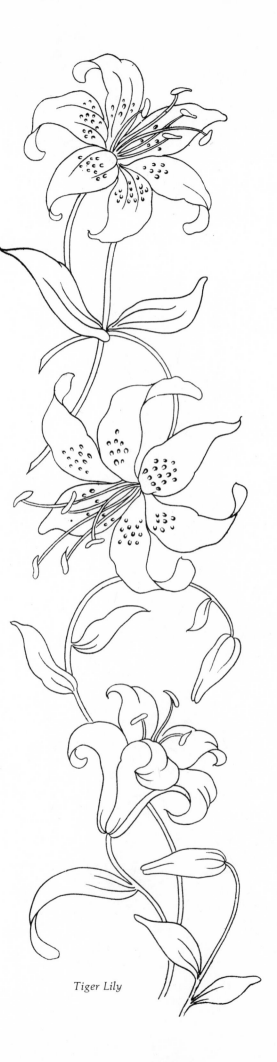

Tiger Lily

Tulip

Sunflower

Apple Blossom

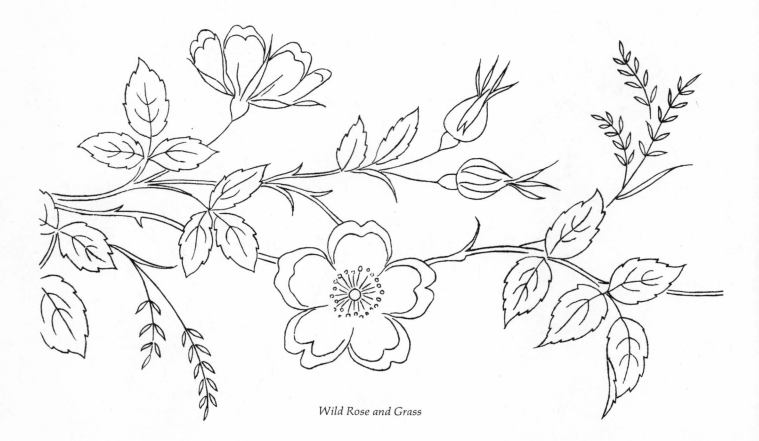

Wild Rose and Grass

Wild Rose

Canterbury Bell

Sweet Pea

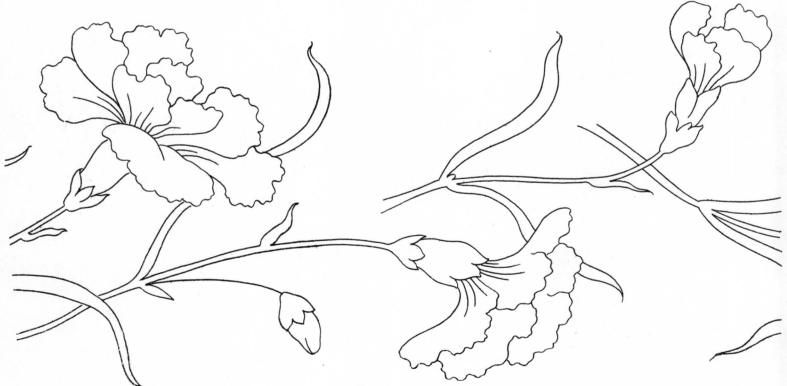

Picotee

Field Poppy and Daisy

Marguerite

Chrysanthemum

Poppy

Ox-Eye Daisy

Tiger Lily

Passion Flower

Single Dahlia

Sunflower

Arum Lily

Nasturtium

Azalea

Vine

Field Poppy and Wheat

Swallows' Flight

Foxglove

Dahlia

Tiger Lily

Marguerite and Palm Fern

Arum Lily

"Bird" Quilt Squares

Beastie Quilt Square

Beastie Quilt Square

Jub-Jub Bird

Wansley Dragon

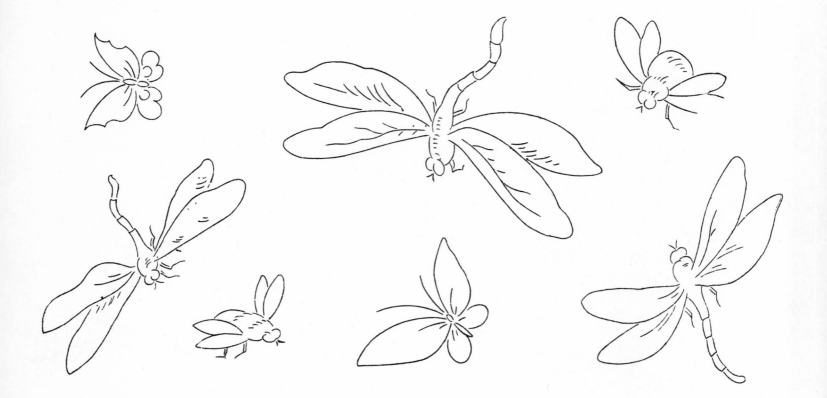

Brook and Willow

Crane

Flamingo

Swan

Stork

Kingfisher

Iris and Water Lily

Index of Motifs